Understanding Karma

Understanding Karma

Rethinking Destiny, Reincarnation and Free Will

Jens Heisterkamp

Floris Books

Translated by Matthew Barton

First published in German as *Karma neu denken: Wiederverkörperung und Schicksal als Herausforderung für die Vernunft* by Info3 Verlag, Stuttgart in 2023
First published in English by Floris Books, Edinburgh in 2025. © 2023 Info3 Verlag
English version © 2025 Floris Books
Jens Heisterkamp has asserted his right under the Copyright, Designs and Patent Act 1988 to be identified as the Author of this Work.
All rights reserved. No part of this book may be reproduced without prior permission of Floris Books, Edinburgh
www.florisbooks.co.uk

Also available as an eBook

Authorised EU Representative: Easy Access System Europe, Mustamae tee 50, 10621 Tallinn, Estonia gpsr.requests@easproject.com
British Library CIP data available
ISBN 978-178250-947-9

Contents

Introduction	7
1. Reincarnation in East and West	14
2. The Challenges Posed by Reincarnation and Karma	26
3. Freedom Seeks Karma	43
4. Karma as Development Not Punishment	55
5. Karma Enhances Human Dignity	62
6. The Way Ahead	71
Notes	75
Bibliography	77

*The human soul
resembles water:
it comes from the heavens,
rises to the heavens,
and must descend
to the earth once more
in an eternal to and fro.*

        Goethe

Introduction

Do we live more than once? Have we lived other lives before our current one, and will there be others when this one is over? To consider this possibility raises many questions. Will I myself come back again? If so, how is that possible? Where will I exist between lifetimes? And why can I not remember anything from before this earthly life? If it is true, it will call into question a great many of our assumptions about our lives and the world we live in.

In the West, reincarnation has often been regarded as an exotic flower of Eastern philosophy or dismissed as a crazy, New Age belief. But over the years it has entered more and more into our culture. David Mitchell's 2004 novel, *Cloud Atlas,* which was later adapted for film, played with the idea that its protagonists return as different characters as the plot unfolds over many centuries – from the South Pacific in the eighteenth century to a distant post-apocalyptic, post-technological future. Other recent films, TV series and publications likewise touch on it. For example, an article in *Focus*

Online in January 2022 carries the header, 'How to Rid Yourself of Bad Karma'; a Frankfurt-based campaign to end child poverty in India calls itself 'Karma Hero'; and Plan International, an organisation that works with children in over eighty countries to build a more equal world, created its first-ever animated Global Ambassador called Karma Grant, an aspiring musician who works to promote the education of young women in developing countries. In other words, the idea of reincarnation and karma has become common currency, even if used in somewhat tongue-in-cheek way. According to a Statista survey carried out in Germany in 2017, 35% of those questioned were convinced they had lived before. Helmut Obst, a religious studies academic who wrote a book called *Reinkarnation: Weltgeschichte einer Idee* (*Reincarnation: The History of an Idea*), speaks of reincarnation as a transreligious concept. Even mainstream adherents of Christianity subscribe to it, as the Protestant theologian Ruediger Sachau discovered in a survey of Swiss congregations in 1998. Today, it seems, more people believe in reincarnation than in the Resurrection.

But popularisation of the idea should not lead us to overlook the fact that this is by no means a simple or straightforward matter; many who feel sympathetic towards such an outlook may not necessarily realise its full ramifications. The idea of reincarnation and karma (or destiny) is still new and unaccustomed in Western culture, not least because it appears to contradict everything we know from empirical science. Many regard the idea as a refuge for those who cannot cope with the complexities of modern life and thus seek solace in a seemingly irrational belief system. Nor does it lend credence to the idea when advocates of reincarnation spend their time speculating about which important historical figure they may have been in a former life, or when they declare, with a total lack of feeling, that the misfortune of others can be explained by their conduct in a past life.

But none of this is implicit in the idea itself. In this book I want to show that there are very valuable grounds for discussing the idea of reincarnation and karma, and I would contest the view that we cannot take it seriously in our scientific era. Markus Gabriel, one of the most highly regarded modern philosophers, writes in his book *Der Mensch als Tier* (*Man as an Animal*):

> Even the belief in reincarnation is not one that science can refute or exclude since the sciences only describe, explain and to some degree predict how processes and structures arise in the universe, yet no conclusion can be drawn from

this that the processes and structures that the sciences investigate are the only ones that exist.[1]

The idea of reincarnation and karma is not 'provable' in the everyday sense, but it is nevertheless one worth examining and testing. The aim of this book is therefore to ask how far we can get by examining the principle of reincarnation and karma from a rational standpoint. It is not concerned with satisfying anyone's curiosity about the past lives of particular personalities, nor with tips as to how one might discover one's own previous incarnations. Anyone wishing to pursue this must look elsewhere. Above all this means that I will endeavour to maintain transparent distinctions between philosophical phenomenology, conceptual conclusions and speculation. I will seek to differentiate between what I can ascertain through my own insights and what I have derived from other sources, most notably the anthroposophy of Rudolf Steiner. Of primary importance in investigating where this idea can lead us is an open, questioning attitude.

But at the outset I believe I can already say this: the idea of reincarnation and karma possesses a hidden potential capable of altering everything we think about our world and ourselves. It is not surprising therefore that it meets with much scepticism, and because of that I'd like to preface these reflections with a personal anecdote. I, too, was initially very sceptical of it. When I began my studies at about the age of twenty, I was looking for meaning and purpose in life. I had little time for philosophy, not least because I had gained the impression from friends who were studying the subject that it was an overly elaborate way of saying that we can never know anything. I thought that if philosophy had something of real importance to say about life, it would have found its way into general discourse. For me this would have included, above all, the question of whether there is any kind of life after death. According to what classmates of mine had said about philosophy, this discipline seemed to hold no answers to such questions.

Then, as I began my university studies, and quite separately from them, I read a book by Rudolf Steiner and my response was quite different. Here was someone with something significant to say about life and who seemed to be saying them *to me*. I felt as though I was being personally addressed by this author whom I had never heard of before. He spoke of the spirit and of a world not identical with physical reality. Rather than drawing on speculative philosophy, it was clear he was describing all of this from personal experience. There is a life, a form of existence, he was saying, that is independent of the physical body. This thought sank deep into my youthful soul.

Subsequently, I found my way to a group of students concerned with philosophy and anthroposophy, and my own understanding of philosophy altered radically. I learned that thinkers such as Plato, Aristotle, Descartes, Fichte and Hegel had produced precise insights into soul and spirit, into the nature of the 'I' or ego, and even into the sphere of a 'world spirit', but that modern philosophy was neither able nor willing to take such insights seriously.

In my view, Steiner's work continued in the stream of these great philosophers, while at the same time developing it further through his own spiritual experiences. I read one book after another and through them an ever-more encompassing worldview gave me new and surprising perspectives on life. Almost everything I read struck me as familiar. I felt a sense of trust in this author, even in relation to things that I could not yet properly grasp or evaluate. Whenever I encountered something that struck me as strange, I nevertheless thought that at some point I would come to understand it better.

But there was one exception. In one of Rudolf Steiner's books, *Theosophy*, I first encountered the idea of reincarnation and immediately took against it.

Despite Steiner's clear and transparent train of thought, I refused to accept it. How could this be true? This individual, myself, who I am here and now, is supposed to have been born in some quite different form, in a different era, perhaps with another gender and in quite a different cultural setting? I am supposed to have lived many times before? I felt an aversion to the thought. For me the whole idea of reincarnation was somehow at odds with Western culture, nor did it seem to belong to Steiner's otherwise clear, philosophical accounts. It seemed to me like an exotic plant that Steiner had transplanted into an environment that was completely wrong for it. Only slowly did I gain an understanding of it, but I cannot deny that it initially appeared to me as an alien principle.

In what follows, it will become apparent how my views on the matter changed and developed.

1. Reincarnation in East and West

The concept of reincarnation has its origins in India, where rebirth (or metempsychosis) plays an important role in the Hindu *Upanishads*. According to Hinduism the immortal soul is born repeatedly, and the way it lives any particular life determines its karma or destiny in a subsequent life. The teachings of Buddha, which emerged in India in the sixth century BC, also include the doctrine of reincarnation and karma. The key idea here is that we must bring the 'wheel of rebirths' to a stop and free ourselves from karma. Helmut Obst, the commentator on religion mentioned in the introduction, writes: 'In Eastern religion the compulsion to be reborn becomes a burden, indeed a curse instigated by the need to make redress, to balance karma.'[1]

Outside India and other Buddhist countries, ideas of reincarnation and karma tend to figure only rarely. For example, in the Near East, the Jewish Kabbalah took up the idea of reincarnation in the teachings of Isaac Luria. In the Hasidic stories collected by Martin Buber there are some specific accounts of reincarnation, and the idea can also be found in some schools of Islamic mysticism.

In Christianity, on the other hand, this idea remained more or less unknown. There are some theologians who believe that there are indications of it in the gospels, comments by Jesus that can be interpreted to mean that John the Baptist is the reborn prophet Elijah, something not necessarily to be dismissed out of hand.[2] But reincarnation has never been a core belief of Christianity, neither in academic theology nor in the everyday life of Christians. There could scarcely be a greater contrast with Indian culture, where, to this day, reincarnation and karma are used by people to explain their woes or good fortune in terms of what happened in previous lives. It is a way both of salving their conscience and as solace for extreme social inequalities. In India, these ideas are associated with a tradition that has endured for millennia, one which, in the popular mind, attributes a simplified and mechanistic lawfulness to the doctrine of rebirth.

In Western culture, by contrast, a strong individualism developed both in Christian confessions and in individualistic philosophies. This created a milieu in which the idea of repeated births made little headway and found little support.

And yet, in ancient Greek, the idea of reincarnation came to the fore in the figure of Empedocles. As far as we know from the few, fragmentary records, Empedocles was convinced that the human soul exists prior to birth and continues after death. He attributed to the great sage Pythagoras, with his 'superhuman knowledge' and 'wealth of spirit', the capacity to 'effortlessly behold his ten or twenty previous lives'.[3] He was also convinced that human conduct has consequences for a subsequent life. According to Plutarch, at any rate, Empedocles believed 'that even those who have not yet been born and those who have died are alive'.[4]

As long as people had some inkling that the human soul possessed a kind of substantiality, it was natural for them to wonder where this essence had been before a person's life on Earth and what would happen to it after this life had ended. But such thoughts were forgotten as early as Aristotle, for whom the soul's pre-existence had no relevance because it was unavailable to actual observation. One of the first true thinkers, Aristotle did not base his philosophical questions on traditions and speculation, but on the descriptions of phenomena and the conclusions he was able to draw from this. On this basis he was unable to make any statements about the existence of a soul or an individual spirit either before birth or after death. Thus, the idea of pre- and post-earthly existence vanished from the main current of philosophical discourse.

Later, in the thirteenth century AD, the theologian Thomas Aquinas expended a great deal of effort in wresting from classical Aristotelianism the possibility for the continuing life of the individual after death. From our modern, more cynical perspective, it can seem that this was done so that the Catholic Church could assert its authority in this world by pointing to a place where, after death, divine judgment would be passed on the individual soul. But this is a simplification. Aquinas also argued that an individualised spirit was part of God's plan for creation, and that this could not therefore simply dissolve into some universal spirit after death, which Aristotle had suggested and Aquinas's contemporary, the Islamic scholar Averroes, continued to assert.[5]

From this point of view, Thomas Aquinas can be seen, in a sense, as an important pioneer of individualism. As the modern era arrived, this individualism accentuated the uniqueness of each person to such an extent that the idea of repeated lives on Earth, in which the individual came back as a different personality, no longer seemed plausible. The emphasis in Western culture on a single earthly life has contributed to a focus on the uniqueness and dignity of human beings. In retrospect, therefore, it makes complete sense that in the West the idea of recurring earthly lives remained unknown or of no account, allowing individualism to develop unhindered. Our whole way of thinking about human rights today, and the development of basic civil rights, can also be traced back to this.

Nevertheless, within this individualistic, Western stream of thought, the idea of reincarnation did resurface. In his book *Wiederholte Erdenleben* (*Repeated Earth Lives*), published in 1967, the anthroposophic theologian Emil Bock unearthed a series of hidden references to early ideas about reincarnation in European culture. One important proponent of the idea was the Italian philosopher and astronomer Giordano Bruno, who was executed by the Church in 1600. According to Bock, when interrogated by the Inquisition, Bruno expressed the view that:

> Just as the soul can live within a body, so it can also live in another body, and can pass over from one body to another, which, if it be not true, is nevertheless probable in the view of Pythagoras.[6]

Other hints and suggestions can be found in the writings of people like the philosopher Friedrich Schlegel and the poet Novalis, although they do not amount to a systematic edifice of thought, nor do they explore the consequences that necessarily follow on from this idea.

But this can be found, at least in outline, in the work of Gotthold Ephraim Lessing, who introduced the principle of reincarnation in his short book *The Education of the Human Race*, published towards the end of his life in 1780. The idea appears right at the end, where Lessing feels his way cautiously through a number of open questions. Lessing's reflections arose in the context of a search for religious tolerance. Lessing was wondering if it would be a good idea for every person to experience the whole spectrum and diversity of religions as an aid to inner growth. In paragraph ninety-three, he asks:

> The path upon which the whole human race arrives at its perfection must be one which (sooner or later) each individual must also have pursued. But can this be in only one, single life? Can a person have been, in the same life, a true Jew and a spiritual Christian? Can he, in this same life, have encompassed both of these

and advanced beyond them? Surely he cannot!
But why could each single person not also have
been present more than once upon this earth?

And shortly after this comes the decisive question:

Why should I not come again as often as I am
able to acquire new insights, new skills? Do I
accomplish so much at one go, that the effort
of returning would have no worth?[7]

With Lessing, therefore, the themes of immortality and evolution become intertwined for the first time, and alongside this, the principle of religious tolerance surfaces. It is remarkable that someone so dedicated to reason and to the values of the Enlightenment should take up this theme. This represents something like a moment of destiny in the idea of reincarnation itself: its rebirth in Europe as it were.

At the end of the nineteenth century, the philosopher Gideon Spicker picked up on Lessing's ideas. Spicker, a deeply religious man who also had a scientific outlook, sought to give to religion a philosophical form that rested on scientific foundations. But what does the idea of reincarnation, which seems so unavailable to scientific proof, have to do with such an aim?

In his book *Lessing's Weltanshcauung* (*Lessing's Worldview*), Spicker made the daring comment that if one were to combine Lessing's thoughts on the soul, evolution and education as expressed in *The Education of the Human Race*, then

> ...the seemingly absurd idea of metempsychosis would transform itself into a rational psychology and cosmology, one possible solely from the perspective of modern science and theoretical speculation.[8]

Why? This professor of philosophy from Münster had neither mystic inclinations nor a preoccupation with far-eastern cultures. His statement was based solely on coherent thought. Spicker was convinced that in so far as one wishes to conceive of any continued existence at all, then one must think of it in terms of metempsychosis or the transmigration of souls as Lessing did. It was clear to Spicker that an existence in the 'afterlife' after only a single life on earth would mean that a human soul would have to remain for eternity in this single condition: either in eternal damnation or eternal bliss, but without any possibility of further development. But, as Lessing writes in his book, it is vital for human beings to gain ever 'new insights and new skills'. Based on these founding principles, which, according to Spicker, constitute Lessing's worldview – that is, coherent individualism, freedom of will, autonomy and the demand for further development – only reincarnation can follow as a consideration of any kind of immortal existence. At the same time, it is true that this perspective on human development and evolution signifies an immense enhancement of the value of individuality.

In his Mystery Dramas, Rudolf Steiner paid tribute to the logical consistency of Gideon Spicker in the character of Dr Strader. Strader is a scientist who initially resists the idea of reincarnation, but, over the course of the four plays, finds himself compelled to embrace it through the inner coherence of his own reflections. For the character of Dr Strader, like Gideon Spicker and Lessing before him, insight into the enigma of individual human capacities plays a decisive role.

In ideas developed from those of Steiner, the anthroposophist Herbert Witzenmann has expressed the view, founded on very thorough, anthropological studies, that every kind of human learning can be traced back to the 'suppression' of our bodily organisation, an expression taken from Steiner. This 'suppression of the human organisation' means, in other words, that all learning is a creative interplay between our spiritual aspect and the reality mediated by our bodies. If we understand this, we will no longer be tempted to regard a person's inherent and unique capacities as a purely genetic predisposition.

Following from Lessing and Spicker, a metamorphosis of the idea of reincarnation becomes apparent in anthroposophy and remains consistent with the principle of individualism. It is wholly consistent with this when Steiner, in his book *Theosophy*, pushes this individualism to an extreme by stating that every human being is, in spiritual terms, 'his or her own species'.[9] A lion is always the offspring of another lion, likewise a human being is the offspring of human beings, but only physically. Spiritually speaking we do not originate from other human beings, but only from ourselves as the continuation of previous forms of manifestation of our own individuality. To put it yet another way, reincarnation represents a lineage, a line of descent founded within itself, of the 'species' that each of us is. In the same way that we must explain the origin of living creatures from previous species, so we explain the unique nature of each human spirit in terms of its own previous forms of manifestation in former lives on earth. There is no more consistent and coherent way to conceive of individualism.

If, to simplify somewhat and mindful of the danger

of stereotyping, I regard this concept as a more 'Western' one, this is because it picks up on Western individualism. At the same time, however, it pushes the idea of individual development to an extreme whilst simultaneously redeeming this extreme: it shows that the purpose of this individual evolution is to increasingly shed the narrow, egocentric nature of individualisation through repeated reincarnations. Whereas the 'Eastern' outlook, at least in its past forms, was more concerned with a cessation, or even extinguishing, of individuality as the goal of all incarnations, the 'Western' version outlined here looks to a maturing of individuality that overcomes the narrowness and disadvantages of individuation, such as preoccupation with self and isolation from the whole.

The first view originates in a past era that still reverberates in us (albeit often more unconsciously), while the other points to a future that will not consciously be attained for a long time. Both are polarities that do, however, have points of intersection: the West, where the idea of reincarnation is still a new one, could develop respect for the ancient, venerable tradition of the East, and learn how a transcendent element can stand fully within the life of a culture. The very fact that this tradition, which goes back thousands of years, still exists in India, and that millions of people still live with this idea as a self-evident reality, is something we can honour. If the idea of reincarnation came to be acknowledged in the West as a possibility at least, then the East could feel itself more deeply understood. From this perspective, reincarnation would offer opportunities for improving global relationships.

If people in the West find the idea of reincarnation problematic, they are still more uncomfortable with the idea of karma: the moral consequences that supposedly extend beyond each individual life. In India this is something entirely accepted. People assume that the conditions and circumstances of their present life can be explained by karmic cause and effect. In the West, on the other hand, such a dimension is almost entirely absent. We know and acknowledge only physical laws, not an objective lawfulness that operates on a spiritual level, let alone a moral one. The scepticism we feel towards such ideas could, however, be a good thing. As I will try to show, karmic causality is not as simple or straightforward a matter as it may at first appear. The intellectual individualism of the West has some advantages in relation to this question since it compels us to question things more closely. This leads to a more cautious and nuanced approach to karma, seeing it not as something rigidly imposed upon us, but rather something in which, at a deeper level, we ourselves participate.

2. The Challenges Posed by Reincarnation and Karma

In today's world, defined as it is by the scientific outlook, the idea of reincarnation and karma remains a marginal one. Even though, as we have seen in the previous chapter, the idea meets with a fairly high degree of sympathy among the general population, the public media and many political organisations regard it with suspicion. The social psychologist Pia Lamberty, in her book *Dangerous Beliefs*, which she coauthored with Katharina Nocun, even attributes some 'inhuman' traits to it, since it can be seen as making people culpable for their own misfortunes. The adherents of the idea are also accused of an irrational and anti-science outlook, which could give rise to undesirable social conduct.

There is no doubt that the idea of reincarnation can be used in a very unthinking and insensitive way. It is also responsible for some people making very trivial claims, such as when they declare they were

Cleopatra in a former incarnation or some other great figure from history.[1] Nevertheless, we saw that the idea has found rational supporters at various points in European cultural history. Unfortunately, the principles of rationality, science and scholarship are usually applied in a very narrow and utilitarian sense: science and reason are seen as valid only in terms of sense-based, demonstrable evidence. This narrower view of science states that only what is physical can be the subject of research. The worldview founded on this, often presented as absolute, finds itself challenged by four aspects of reincarnation and karma, which will be considered in the following sections.

First challenge: an immortal individuality is reincarnated

The principle of reincarnation and karma, or destiny, is embedded in the assumption that something in us survives death. But in the natural-scientific worldview, which seeks to explain all phenomena by reducing them to what can be empirically proven, such a thing is not possible. We live in an age in which all that we are is understood materially: our body is explained by genetics, our feelings by psychology and our consciousness by neurology. From our genome to our brain's synapses, nothing remains that is not explicable in purely materialistic terms. The assumption must therefore be dismissed out of hand that there is something in us that survives physical death, some essential aspect of our being that was present in a different form before this life began and which will again seek a new embodiment after death. Natural science does not regard our 'I' or ego as having an independent existence, but as an illusory phenomenon that appears within our consciousness (which natural science itself considers to be an epiphenomenon arising from an increasingly complex but wholly material process). But it is precisely this 'illusory phenomenon' that the idea of reincarnation is concerned with.

Let us try to bring this 'something' into clearer focus. This requires an act of introspection made somewhat easier by the experience of contemplation and meditation. To begin with, we focus our attention on the fleeting, intangible and yet ever-present entity that constitutes our conscious mind. It is not a matter of reflecting on the nature of consciousness or on how it can be explained – consciousness is always present; it is pure presence that precedes all perception and reflection. If I maintain this awareness of myself, irrespective of any particular content or thought, this can lead me to the insight that such self-awareness cannot be explained by anything outside of itself. As I meditatively survey the conscious mind itself, my 'I-being' can manifest as a self-sustaining condition. This experience of the self gives an inner certainty that dismisses every attempt at reductionism. And this leads in turn to the thought that this self is more than a theoretical potential: it has a personal hue that makes it precisely my own self and no one else's. Above all, this self is also the starting point for entirely individual abilities that characterise my distinctive and unique being.

Our skills and abilities, but also our limitations, say a great deal about us. Already in young children these appear in their diverse and distinctive mix. Here is just one example among many others. The sculptor Wilhelm Lehmbruck was born in 1881 to a large, impoverished miner's family that offered nothing in the way of artistic stimulus. A genius for drawing and sculpture was only discovered in the boy thanks to his sensitive and perceptive primary school teacher. The teacher supported his young pupil in his artistic endeavours and eventually arranged a grant for the young Wilhelm to go to the art academy. Wilhelm Lehmbruck became a forerunner of modern sculpture, an important influence on Joseph Beuys among others. The scientific mind will naturally point here to a particular genetic predisposition to explain Lehmbruck's genius for drawing, painting and sculpture. But this merely pushes the mystery of such a gift into deeper obscurity.

That our gifts and individual character are fundamentally mysterious is of course true for every person, not just outstanding talents. But such manifest gifts point to the core of our individuality that cannot be explained solely by external or environmental factors. It seems, if we study this carefully, that everyone brings certain endowments with them at birth.

The versatile thinker Ken Wilber looks suggest something similar when he writes:

> Whatever one may think about reincarnation, it does at least explain one of the most confusing facts encountered by developmental psychologists, and never satisfactorily explained by them: some people grow up under ideal circumstances, with more or less perfect parents, and still develop in dysfunctional ways. Other people by contrast are born into the most difficult circumstances and yet develop normally, sometimes even in extraordinary ways.[2]

How do our skills and abilities normally arise?

Learning always occurs in a specific cultural context, and can often be an arduous process. Learning to write or use tools, for instance, only comes about when we overcome certain forms of resistance. Speaking very generally, the essence of every new skill we learn is a process in which an irreducible self – always a given – engages in a reciprocal relationship with external factors. But if every individual begins their path in life with certain potential abilities, it is easy to see how these abilities might be an innate predisposition from before this present life began, the fruits of former experiences from a former life, which are then reconfigured into the talents and inclinations we see in this life.

Second challenge: heaven is here

The idea that 'something' reincarnates is not enough by itself for us to understand the overall picture. We must also ask *how* this happens. We must rethink the whole of reality if reincarnation exists. A dimension between death and rebirth is required in which, after death, we develop further as immortal individuals, freeing ourselves from hindrances and preparing ourselves for new tasks. To put it in metaphorical and traditional terms, a 'heaven' is needed, a purely spiritual world of pure spirits. There are exceptions to this in some cultures. In

Tibetan Buddhism, for example, it is believed that the individuality of the Dalai Lama reincarnates immediately at death into a child who must then be discovered and confirmed by those who know the signs.

But for most of us, an existence between death and rebirth is required before we reincarnate, one that is continually interwoven with earthly reality. This must mean that there is a continual presence of purely spiritual powers on the earth where we dwell, working so that karma can take effect in our lives with its new opportunities. It may be that 'this side' and 'the other side' are not nearly as different as we suppose; perhaps they are more like two sides of one, all-encompassing reality. This is an idea at odds with many traditional views of the afterlife. But how does our reincarnating soul-spirit find its way to parents who enable us to pursue our further journey? And what about that well-known phenomenon of synchronicity, in which seemingly chance meetings bring us into contact with souls who are deeply familiar to us from long ago and who participate in the workings of karma? How do these so-called 'chance' events arise ('chance' being something the theologian Albert Schweitzer called the 'pseudonym God chooses when he wishes to remain incognito')?

Examples of such 'chance' encounters are familiar

2. THE CHALLENGES POSED BY REINCARNATION AND KARMA

to all of us from our own lives or the lives of those close to us. History furnishes us with even more examples. One famous instance relates to the explorer Christopher Columbus. Despite his connections to the Spanish royal family, he received no support for a planned expedition to prove that, because the earth is round, there was a sea route to India. During a trip to France, and feeling resigned to the impossibility of ever raising funds, Columbus met a Franciscan monk who was a confidant of Queen Isabella of Spain. The monk offered to compose a letter of appeal to her, which subsequently turned out to be successful. Columbus was invited to the court and a little while later was able to embark on his famous voyage of exploration. Would this have been possible otherwise? His powerful urge to explore and discover new lands might not have been realised if not for this fateful encounter, which led to Spain's major involvement in colonial history, however deplorable we now regard it.

Of course, very few of our own biographical turning points have historical significance, but we can still regard them as 'destined' moments, even without considering their profounder aspects. But the more we reflect on such contexts and connections, the more insistently the question may arise for us as to the nature of a reality that enables such things to occur. How does a 'higher self' construct our destiny? We do not manage all of this on our own, surely? If karma is at work, it presupposes a living world on the 'other side', and on 'this side' a world pervaded by spirit in which spiritual beings are constantly at work. A part must also be played by the so-called dead who are certainly living amongst us on 'this side'. They are part of the whole fabric of reality, not only in so far as we think about them and remember them, but also by being interwoven with our daily life in a spiritually real sense.

The writer Thornton Wilder once used the image of a woven rug as a metaphor for the reality of our lives: on its upper side, corresponding to our everyday consciousness, we see meaningful patterns and forms, but when we turn it over we see a tangle of knots and criss-cross threads.[3] This may be one way to think of the dynamic activities continually at work beneath the surface of our life. But many questions remain open and unresolved in this realm.

Third challenge: evolution as the meaning of reincarnation

The next assumption consists in the meaningfulness of everything. The point of reincarnation and karma lies in our evolution towards greater perfection, which, as we saw, is a thought that Lessing had already introduced. Spicker, an important interpreter of Lessing's work, reminds us that this is necessarily implied by the 'principle of evolution':

> Immortality can be assumed only on the condition that the human being, and indeed each individual human being, is called upon to achieve a higher degree of moral and spiritual perfection than has been possible in this life.[4]

Rudolf Steiner put it a similar way in one of his lectures:

> Thus, for the sake of our own progress, we can really only wish that there is karma as objective justice.[5]

If we see in the process of reincarnation and karma the workings of a higher wisdom (perhaps also the higher wisdom of our own higher being), then we begin to understand that in this current life we face the consequences of our own past deeds in order that we can grow by this experience. Put generally, we are faced with the need to further shape and configure the tapestry of connections between our fellow human beings. Such elaboration requires more than a single lifetime, more even than several lifetimes.

According to Steiner, this process will take the lifetime of our Earth to be completed, and this seems realistic given that the goal of elaboration and resolution of all personal karma cannot be a short-term one. It does, however, help to shed light on some of the self-involved terminology found in 'self-improvement' groups, with their emphasis on 'self-sufficiency'. Achieving something for ourselves is more appealing than being reliant on others, but karma presents us with a very different perspective on this.

How can we characterise the goal of this evolution more precisely? Although we cannot give a concrete description of the steps that will take us in this direction, in general we can say that they will involve an ever-increasing process of human individuation. Through this we will introduce something entirely new into the world: the universal spirit that is the origin and foundation of everything that exists, but which has now been assimilated and penetrated through by each individual person. At the same time, through the workings of karma, we will develop an ever-increasing capacity for community: we will learn in a fundamental sense what it means to be social beings. Karma is therefore not merely one aspect or a single element of a worldview, but an encompassing outlook on life, integral to which is the goal of freedom within connection and relatedness.

Fourth challenge: there is an objective moral structure to the world

Perhaps the most challenging assumption is that the workings of karma presuppose something like a morally oriented structure to the world, which, however this may manifest in particular circumstances, nevertheless involves the principle of establishing or re-establishing balance. The idea that our many incarnations are founded on the existence of a superordinate, objective, moral perspective – and therefore one not encompassed by our personal preferences and societal conventions – understandably throws up questions. Why should the world be organised in this way? Doesn't the evidence of our eyes and our experience of life negate the very idea that there is an 'objective morality' at work in the world?

On closer examination, however, we discover that certain elements of moral recompense are more familiar to us than we may think. Without even seeing this in terms of karma, we continually live our lives in a way that takes for granted ideas such as giving and taking, fault and redress. But outside of the legal domain, most people react almost allergically to ideas of 'fault', 'debt' or 'guilt'. We object to owing anything to anyone, or to be indebted in any way. And yet we certainly owe a debt to our parents, for instance; we owe our lives to them and, in ideal circumstances, it was they who helped prepare us for our own life to the best of their abilities. While we don't have to keep this 'debt' continually in mind, we can still express gratitude to our parents and caregivers for all they have done for us. To be aware that we owe something to others is therefore entirely different from feeling guilt.

I think that relationships of moral recompense and rebalancing are an anthropological reality deeply rooted in interpersonal life: one friend gives me a helpful piece of advice, another friend helps me in a difficult situation. I feel grateful and beholden to them, and I would gladly recompense them in some way if I can. This is a basic need of social dynamics. It is even true when someone gives us something without any expectations attached to the gift: we still feel bound to give them something in return.

It therefore seems to me that we cannot avoid the interplay of giving and taking, of debt and recompense. These two poles are connected and strive continually for balance. This holds true in ordinary life between birth and death, but could it not also apply above and

2. THE CHALLENGES POSED BY REINCARNATION AND KARMA

beyond this present life?

Specifically, this would mean that if I do a good deed to someone, it will have consequences not only in this life but in further encounters beyond it. Likewise, a hurtful action will need to be redressed in some form in a subsequent life. How exactly such redress might happen is usually beyond our understanding, and we should be careful not to take the idea of recompense in a purely mechanical way, such that like is always repaid by like. After all, two wrongs still do not make a right even in matters of karma.

Nevertheless, in an era in which all phenomena are attributed to physical causes , such an idea is especially alien. To assume consequences of our conduct after death strikes many as peculiar, although it is not so outlandish as it may at first sound. We find something like this in almost all religions. Judaism, Christianity and Islam all entertain the idea that we will be held to account for our actions at the end of time and that God, as the highest authority of justice, will judge our actions accordingly. The Gospel of Matthew speaks of a Last Judgement:

> But I tell you that everyone will have to give account on the day of judgment for every empty word they have spoken. For by your words you

will be acquitted, and by your words you will be condemned. (Matt. 12:36–37)

Many other similar passages could be cited. And we are all probably familiar with the striking representation of Christ as world judge in Michelangelo's famous ceiling in the Sistine Chapel.

The image of a God who ordains consequences for moral failings, however, seems at odds with the 'God of love'. Indeed, the very idea of judgement seems to be the preserve of more fundamentalist outlooks. Nevertheless, simply dismissing the idea of judgement is inconsistent. If there were to be no redress or recompense for immoral or moral deeds, the world would lack an essential element: justice. At least for a believer, it seems unacceptable that SS murderers or fanatic suicide bombers should be received by God with the same love as the victims of such actions. To conceive of a deeper moral redress seems a necessity in a creation to which we attribute divine justice of some kind.

The philosopher Holm Tetens sees this idea in the broader context of *redemption*, which surpasses mere recompense and punishment. He writes:

Without the idea of judgement as an inherent

precondition of forgiveness and reconciliation, redemption would be a process that did not take human beings seriously as rational, responsible people. Those, therefore, who wish to avoid talk of judgement, should also be silent on the idea of redemption.[6]

Tetens even outlines a transcendental configuration in which, at the end of creation, God gathers the dead together to confront them with the consequences of their actions and to enact a kind of perpetrator-victim redress:

God can think the life of these people further by conceiving of them as being reincarnated in a 'new body'. If people are to encounter one another again, be reconciled with one another and lead a fulfilled life together, God will in fact be obliged to reincarnate them in a 'new body'.[7]

Tetens's conclusion here is astonishing. But what he has arrived at through a process of thinking logically and consequentially can easily be applied to the principle of reincarnation and karma. Here, there is no divine 'court' nor any reconciliation 'within' God, but rather a redress chosen by people themselves in a real body in a real, future life. It is we human beings ourselves who – albeit not in our everyday awareness, but out of a higher consciousness that we possess between death and rebirth – find ourselves confronted after every incarnation with the consequences of our previous conduct and, desiring to make redress for it, seek out circumstances in a subsequent life that will make redemption possible.

In a lecture he gave in 1910, Rudolf Steiner gave a simple instance of this:

> Let us assume for instance that somebody died at the age of seventy and lives their life backwards to their fortieth year, when they struck someone in the face. They then experience the pain they caused the other. This produces a kind of self-reproach; from this the person retains a longing which they take into their next life – a longing to make good this deed in their next life.[8]

But we must not see this in simplistic, purely punitive terms, such that in a following life the perpetrator receives a punch to the face themselves. Steiner also spoke of a 'corresponding good deed' through which redress can occur.[9]

3. Freedom Seeks Karma

We now come to the next of our propositions: karma does not stand in opposition to freedom; on the contrary, it follows from it if we take freedom seriously. Karma can only be at odds with freedom if we understand (or rather *mis*understand) it to be a purely mechanistic form of causality, a chain of imperative consequences. But as human beings we are free; that is, our nature is characterised by the ability to adopt ever new approaches towards the necessary conditions of our lives and to exercise our free will. There is no closed chain of cause and effect. As free beings we also bear responsibility for the consequences of our actions, for everything we undertake or omit to do, and we must measure – and be measured by – the degree to which we meet our responsibilities. If this were not so, we would not be free. This is already true of life between birth and death, but now comes another important step: karma carries this principle of responsibility beyond a single life.

Extending responsibility beyond one lifetime counteracts a certain critique of the concept of freedom that has often been cited in recent times. Those who think of freedom only in terms of doing whatever you like, criticise what they regard as the desire to lead a self-centred life with little regard for the wellbeing of others or the consequences of our actions. Even without adopting a spiritual perspective on the matter, this view fails to do justice to the real dignity of freedom. I bear responsibility *because* I am free. If we then extend this by including the idea of karma, it becomes clearer still: freedom has consequences beyond this one life for my own future and that of my fellow human beings. What we resolve to do in freedom, or decide not to do, remains connected with us and will return to us in some form.

In his book *Theosophy*, Steiner writes: 'In the effects of its actions, the human soul lives on in a second independent life.'[1] The traces of our actions are inscribed in the physical world, but how can the consequences of these actions return to us in a completely different era under entirely different circumstances? During life between birth and death this is a straightforward matter: if I do not pay my taxes, then at some point the tax office will track me down and demand that I pay what I owe. So what happens when not only a great deal of time elapses between death and a new birth, but

3. FREEDOM SEEKS KARMA

we are also born in an entirely different place and set of circumstances? In *Theosophy*, by way of a comparison, Steiner provides the example of moving from one country to another:

> If my field of activity is shifted from Europe to America, I will also find myself in totally new surroundings, and yet my life in America will still be quite dependent on how I used to live in Europe. If I was a mechanic in Europe, my life in America will take shape quite differently than it would if I was a banker. In the first instance, I will probably be surrounded by machinery again in America; in the second, by the trappings of the banking business.[2]

According to Steiner this happens because:

> In each case, my former life determines my surroundings; it extracts from the entire surrounding world those things that are related to it, so to speak.[3]

This answer remains somewhat theoretical unless we can, in Thornton Wilder's phrase, turn the 'carpet' over and look at its reverse side.

Cause and effect

Every cause has an effect. This is true both in the natural world and in human life, and wherever we find an effect, we can look for a cause. As long as we confine ourselves to a single lifetime, causality seems straightforward and uncontradictory. If I have a poor diet, this has consequences for my health. If I treat others badly, they will distance themselves from me. I will find myself in court if I break the law, and if justice is properly dispensed and I end up in prison, I can say that it is 'my own fault'. Few will object to such a statement.

But how might it appear if the effects of human conduct extended beyond a single life on earth? If the consequences of the freedom I exercised in a former life came back to me again in a subsequent one? It must be said straight away that the basis for judging such instances will be quite different from earthly laws and judgements. There are fixed laws relating to physical and social reality that underlie cause and effect in ordinary life: a linking of conduct, culpability, responsibility and punishment, and clear rules according to which the logic of legality works. Such a logic does not necessarily apply in the same way in the case of reincarnation and karma, and it would be a mistake to project this comparatively simplistic structure of the law upon the workings of a quite different sphere. We cannot even discern what is cause and what is effect in any one event, and we definitely should not ascribe everything that happens to us or to someone else as the consequences of something we or they may have done. We might be tempted, out of a certain habit of thought, to apply the logic of legality to karma, but this simply does not function here. Nor, as I will show later in more detail, does a conventional 'religious logic' function here either: the idea that human happiness can be explained as God's reward for good deeds, and human suffering as his punishment for bad ones.

Karma follows a quite different kind of 'logic', if we can even call it that. It is neither a matter of legalistic redress nor some supposed 'divine law', both of which are products of a rational though limited comprehension. Rather, karma has to do with a wisdom beyond justice, religion and rationality. It is hidden from us behind a veil of unknowing that, in cultural-historic terms, we have only recently become aware of and are still very far from lifting.

What we can say for sure is this: in the 'logic' of reincarnation and karma our free, responsible 'I' plays a key role. However grand it sounds, we must assume that morality is an organising principle of the whole cosmos. But it is important to understand that this principle is not governed by divine powers alone, as religions assert, but that it is we ourselves who want to make amends for the errors of a past life and continue the process of development we are engaged in. We rediscover each other over and again – our loved ones but also our adversaries, our teachers and our victims. What a breathtaking prospect this is. If true, then karma as a principle of balance would be a world-sustaining pattern into which we human beings are incorporated – both in our present life, with its daily moments of destiny, and beyond the threshold in the life between death and a new birth where we prepare for our next incarnation. This would mean that evolution, individualisation and striving for freedom within an interlinked network of human beings is the fundamental purpose of the universe.

Herbert Witzenmann, whom we cited earlier, goes as far as to assume that the principle of reincarnation is itself undergoing an evolution corresponding to the development of human consciousness. In a very interesting conversation with Henning Koehler, he once pointed to a comment by Rudolf Steiner according to which (with a few, notable exceptions) we can only speak of repeated earthly lives in the full, individual sense, since the fifteenth century. In other words, since the human being has acquired the capacity for inner self-observation of thinking. Previously it was more a matter of reincarnating into groups and communities with a collective destiny. In a certain sense, therefore, we are now entering upon reincarnation as beings with self-knowledge.[4]

This surprising comment can help us understand reincarnation and karma as something that manifests through us and for us rather than as something we passively suffer.

No mechanical causality

This approach helps us to counter the idea that karma operates in a purely fatalistic way. No matter how fundamental the karmic principle of cause and effect may appear, individual cases will always be complex, and our ability to fully comprehend such complexity is likely to be limited. I cannot necessarily judge whether the events in my life are the consequences of a former life, and the matter is even less clear given that I am continually affected by the actions of other people. If, for instance, someone attacks me and steals something from me, this does not have to be caused by something in my karmic past. I have not necessarily brought this event upon myself by my past actions. Since freedom exists, I and others can perform new, un-predetermined actions at every moment, thus creating new causes with their good and bad consequences. From this perspective, the person who attacks me is (quite apart from any legal repercussions) creating new karma for themselves. At some point in the future they will be confronted by the consequences of their action so that a rebalancing can occur. This being so, their criminal action in no way arises as a necessary effect of a past cause, but its consequences nevertheless reverberate on into the future. I cannot know what these consequences will be, however. Steiner asserts that, 'whether an experience of the human being is the effect of his karmic past or the cause of his karmic future will have to be determined in every individual instance'.[5]

Steiner also states that some people see things too simplistically, for instance believing that:

> ...if a tile falls on their head, they must have karmically deserved this injury. But this is by no means necessarily so. In the life of every human being, events continually occur that have nothing to do with their good or bad deeds in the past. Such events will find their karmic redress in the future.[6]

Karma is not a closed, causal chain originating in the past, which would assume a completely mechanistic worldview. If every event were to be merely the consequence of another, it would have to be balanced by yet another in turn, signifying a never-ending chain of events and a fixed, narrow determinism.

Buddha himself clearly objected to this view since it equated to fatalism. In his era, for example, the Brahmins used the principle of karma to legitimise the caste system:

> In extreme instances, people thought that whatever happened to someone in their present life was the effect of past actions. Gautama criticised this outlook: if everything were determined by previous causes, he said, this would also apply to any intentional action done in the present moment, in which case every free endeavour for further self-development would be pointless if all were already pre-ordained … Those who explained their present circumstances and their actions as the effects of former deeds were regarded by Gautama as people living *without spiritual clarity and self-mastery*, who preferred a mechanistic worldview to acknowledgement that deeds could be done anew in each moment.[7]

Unfortunately, our rational mind has a strong affinity with mechanistic thinking. If people believe they possess higher insight into karmic connections when they see victims as culpable for their own suffering, then they are in fact seeing things only in a very partial, reductive and therefore mistaken way.

Karma and empathy

To develop a feeling for one's own destiny, Rudolf Steiner suggests looking back on a series of events in our own life – even if they are painful ones – as if we ourselves had 'arranged' them. For example, let's say someone I love leaves me. To begin with, I can't understand it. I refuse to accept the separation and suffer from the loss. A long, bitter time ensues.

Only much later, when I look back on this period, can I perhaps recognise that the person I loved had quite different ideas about life than I did. They had reasons for going. But they might also have provided me with an opportunity. As a result of the separation I am able to pursue certain interests with a much greater intensity. They even become the determining focus of my whole life. If the person in question had not left me back then, my life could not have taken the direction it did. From my present perspective, it even seems meaningful that they left me, as if I myself could not have wished for anything else. At the level of ordinary awareness, I would not have wanted the separation, I would have fiercely resisted it. But the factors at work in karma are superconscious ones, beyond our everyday consciousness.

Whether I inflicted something upon myself, and if so, whether I can accept this, is a key question that no outer authority can determine. To tell someone else that 'You wanted this, it is your karma', is not only insensitive but is devoid of a deeper understanding since such situations cannot be judged by others. Here it can be helpful to reflect on the differentiated outlook of therapist Renate Hoelzer-Hasselberg who once said the following in an interview:

> Ultimately, what Viktor Frankl once said holds true here: 'So what is the human being? We are beings who always decide what we are.' People who at some point succeed in letting go of resistance, of assigning culpability, of wishing they had done things differently, and who instead can cultivate a profound sense that 'This is connected with me', will find that something in them changes. Then, perhaps, they may also come to consider that karma is

always benevolent ... You can't impose this on anyone, which would be terrible if they are suffering a lot, and it wouldn't be a good thing in therapy either. To tell someone what they should think or do, above all when they are in pain, almost always means that we do not wish to engage in an emotional relationship with them. We then take flight from the empathy and compassion that is required into more abstract manners of expression and modes of behaviour. We apply a formula, and while this may be true in itself, it is no substitute for relationship. Only I can say to myself, when I come to the point of being able to do so, that my karma is good. I can perhaps recognise, 'I'm suffering, I did not think I wanted this, but in a sense perhaps I did because it is connected with my own development.'[8]

A true understanding of karma, therefore, does not promote an unfeeling aloofness towards our fellow human beings, which has nothing to do with true spirituality or esotericism.

4. Karma as Development Not Punishment

Reincarnation and karma unfold in a dimension of living wisdom that is unavailable to intellectual or emotional judgements. If I take this seriously, I should be cautious with some recorded statements by Rudolf Steiner about karma and illness, which should not be seen in a formulaic or dogmatic way. Here and there Steiner spoke about how certain (and by no means all!) illnesses have a karmic cause. For instance, here:

> Thus we can karmically trace the effects in three consecutive incarnations: superficiality and unsteadiness in the first incarnation, the tendency to lying in the second, and the physical disposition to illness in the third incarnation. This shows us how karma is connected with health and illness.[1]

Such connections between moral deficiencies and a tendency towards illness in a subsequent incarnation may well exist, but the question remains as to how I myself deal with this. Certainly, the field of psychosomatics is familiar with connections between inner attitudes and their physical expression, and it is conceivable that such a thing could work on into a future incarnation. But we should keep in mind that such statements should not be thought of in terms of a quasi-mechanical 'lawfulness'. For me personally, inner honesty demands that I do not circulate as doctrine comments that I cannot verify myself or use them to form judgements about other people. Fundamentally, engagement with the idea of karma is for me such an intimate and sensitive matter that any outer diagnosis by another seems misplaced.

Rudolf Steiner also offered varied reflections on the origins of illness. In a different context he said that a human soul may have experienced such terrible things in a previous life that, at the moment of connecting with a new body before birth, it hesitates and cannot take proper hold of that body. One consequence of this can be a brain that is restricted in the way it functions.[2] In such a case, the condition would indeed be connected with a previous life, but *not* in a way that would suggest it was caused by the individual.

With Rudolf Steiner, therefore, who more than

anyone else in the twentieth century worked to bring reincarnation to general awareness, we must always remember that he has at least two views of everything. For instance, he also says this:

> This is why we should never really be entirely satisfied with a merely trivial view of illness as something we attract to ourselves through karma. This is because we ought not merely to consider the karma of the past, thus seeing illness as a conclusion, but instead regard illness – which is only a secondary phenomenon – as the developing cause of our future creative power and capacity.

This means that an illness can harbour an unconscious future resolve that will be needed for a particular task in a future life. Steiner goes on:

> We misunderstand illness and karma entirely if we always only consider the past, thereby making karma a more or less completely random law of destiny. Karma becomes a law of action, of life's fruitfulness, however, if we are able to look through the lens of present karma into the future.[3]

Something very similar becomes apparent in another comment by Steiner:

> It is not right to throw everything back to the past. The right attitude to karma leads us to say: 'An illness which befalls me now, need not necessarily be the consequence of earlier weaknesses of soul; it is possible that an illness may constitute a first beginning. Karma holds good, nevertheless.' [4]

Illness and disability

Some critics fear that 'karmic diagnoses' could be used as a form of discrimination against people with special needs, as though they themselves were at fault for their condition. We have already seen how misplaced this is. Anthroposophists have been accused of regarding illnesses or disabilities as karmic 'punishment', and this invites justified criticism since such a view would indeed be uncompassionate. For instance, Dietrich Krauss, author and editor of the TV programme *Die Anstalt* (*The Asylum*), said in a Heinrich Böll *Foundation* podcast in October 2022 that:

> ... there are anthroposophic institutions for

special educational needs that regard disability as a punishment for misconduct in a previous life. This is such an inhumane ideology, and I consider it irresponsible to entrust such people with the care of those with special educational needs.

Unfortunately, while we might respond to this remark with indignation and outrage, it is not inconceivable that such a view of karma might indeed prevent people from cultivating a genuine relationship with those in need of help. But Steiner never uses the term 'punishment' in connection with karma, for karma never 'punishes'. Secondly, and still more importantly, Steiner himself expressly warned against any view of karma that is lacking in compassion:

> An anthroposophist must be clear that the karma of [other] people has no bearing on his own actions towards them, and that he must not withhold help because – in a trivial sense – he believes in karma and therefore thinks that a person brought this fate upon himself. Karma in fact calls on us to help others, since we can be certain that our help signifies something for them that will be

inscribed in their karma and guide it in a more favourable direction. *An understanding of the world founded on karma must lead to compassion.* [my emphasis].[5]

This makes it clear that including the idea of karma in our outlook can increase our capacity for empathy.

The accusation of a belief in illness as 'punishment' might also be a projection, for the idea of punishment by a higher power or deity was, and perhaps still is, deeply rooted in many religions, including orthodox Christianity. I myself once encountered the view, in a Protestant milieu, that parents were being 'punished by God' if they gave birth to a child with special educational needs.

In the past such ideas were even more deeply embedded. For instance, the Gospel of John relates the story of the healing of a man born blind. When the disciples who are with Jesus pass this man, they ask him: 'Rabbi, who sinned, this man or his parents, that he was born blind?' The question shows us that people once saw a self-evident connection between a physical ailment and a moral deficiency. Indeed, one of the causes proposed by the disciples demonstrates a belief in reincarnation, for if it is not the parents who sinned but the young man himself, then this must have been prior to his being born blind. But Jesus replies in a way that completely removes any thought of transgression from this particular instance: 'Neither this man nor his parents sinned … but this happened so that the work of God might be displayed in his life' (John 9:1–3). This 'work of God' is then what occurs when Christ heals the man. Yet this does not have to signify that God 'arranged' this destiny of blindness so that Jesus' power could become manifest through the healing. Jesus simply describes what he is doing, his tangible intervention, whereby healing makes the 'work of God' manifest. He says nothing at all about any prior *cause* of the blindness.

In general, karma's connection with past actions is over-emphasised. If I have ill-treated someone in a former life, I will seek to make redress for this when an opportunity subsequently presents itself. But this does not mean that because I did wrong, wrong will then be done to me in return. No, redress can also mean that I do something good for someone who suffered previously from my actions.

5. Karma Enhances Human Dignity

Having outlined the possibility of reincarnation and karma as far as this can be done, I now want to ask a very simple question: what benefit does this outlook have in daily life? Even if we entertain these ideas as a possibility, are they not, at most, a matter of private, personal significance? Do they have any meaning beyond our own personal interest?

I believe they do. I think that the idea of reincarnation harbours the potential to enhance our social relationships. The foundation of all modern thinking about society is respect for the freedom of the other, which is encapsulated in the laws of many countries in the concept of inalienable human dignity. In other words, every individual embodies an absolute and intrinsic worth that should not be reduced to purely relative or utilitarian terms.

Given its absolute and definitive nature, this intrinsic value needs no further justification. But it seems to

5. KARMA ENHANCES HUMAN DIGNITY

me that it can be inwardly enhanced by the idea of reincarnation. The dignity of the individual becomes still more precious if we add to it the dimension of reincarnation. One can hardly conceive of a greater appreciation of the value of human individuality than to speak of it, as Steiner does, as a 'species in itself' (see Chapter 2).

But here an objection might be raised. Doesn't the perspective of many earthly lives relativise the value of each specific individual life? If death is no longer a final boundary but a transition into further existence, doesn't this diminish the worth of a single human life? I think we have to take this objection seriously, since the significance of this single human life must certainly not be diminished. Whenever we witness the death of someone we love, we inevitably experience the finality of every death from our own earthly perspective. It has to be like this. We rightly grieve for our loss, something that is intrinsic to our humanity. To simply say, 'This soul will be born again in a future life' strikes a sentimental and inappropriate note if it suppresses justified grief.

At the same time, something else is true too, which I would like to illustrate with something that threw up a striking question for me. There is a wonderful documentary about the renowned translator Svetlana

Geier, who, among other things, translated all of Dostoyevsky's great works into German. She had to cope with a difficult family destiny; in particular, she lost her beloved father, from whom she had learned German in Kiev, who was killed by the Soviet apparatchicks. She worked for the Germans during the Second World War and when the German army retreated from Ukraine, she had to move to Berlin for safety. The film, *The Woman with the 5 Elephants*, makes clear how her unusual life experiences flowed into her extraordinary work as a translator.

By the time I saw the film, Svetlana Geier had died. But as I watched it, I found myself questioning how the wonderfully humane person she became could simply have ceased to exist, to have been swallowed up by nothingness again. It suddenly seemed to me – however odd the term may sound here – 'uneconomical' from a larger perspective that such personal human qualities should arise in the world only to fade again into nothing like a beautiful flower. My feelings about this person could equally apply to numerous other figures, such as Dietrich Bonhoefer or Mother Teresa, for example. Such flowerings of the human spirit surely cannot simply disappear into nothing again! Yet this feeling is not limited to outstanding individuals. The feelings elicited in me by the life of Svetlana Geier can naturally surface in relation to many others who have died. Ultimately, we can find something that flowers in every human being and can ask where it survives apart from in the memory of others.

The profound comment Goethe made to the poet Johann Peter Eckermann comes to mind:

> The conviction that our existence continues arises for me from the idea of work and activity. You see, if I work on tirelessly to my end, nature is obliged to assign me a different form of existence when my spirit is no longer able to endure this present one.[1]

And in a conversation with the writer Johannes Daniel Falk, he said something similar:

> I am certain that, as the person you see before you, I have been here a thousand times before and hope to return a thousand times in the future.[2]

If it is true that the essence of a human being does not disappear at death, but that the qualities we have developed work on both for ourselves and for the world, transformed into new capacities and gifts, this would not only be comforting but deeply meaningful. Of course, we should remember that both of these – comfort and meaning – cannot be the basis for accepting the idea of reincarnation. It is also true to say that people of religious sensibility can also find deep solace without believing in reincarnation at all.

Nevertheless, and without overriding these objections, I want to add another thought here connected to the theme of consolation. As we have seen, the hope or expectation of divine justice plays an important role in religions in relation to the profound injustices in the world – not least those inflicted on people by others. So many lives are brutally and randomly cut short. In view of such suffering in the world, the question of theodicy has always been raised – that is, how can a loving God allow such evil to exist in the world? Here the idea of rebirth opens up a new perspective, which, with all due caution, I want to offer as a possibility. If we enter upon a new life that succeeds this one, the suffering of pain and arbitrary death would not be a last, senseless event. All these lives cut short would not vanish into the void, and what they have suffered cannot in fact violate their innermost being. They will have a future; there is hope, for they will return.

Let us say this plainly: such a thought does not in any way detract from their suffering, nor does it, if they are the victims of violence, diminish the responsibility of the perpetrators. In no way does it justify what has been done to them. It does not lend their suffering any retrospective 'meaning'. That would be presumptuous. But it does offer the kind of solace religious people find in the belief that each person, with all their pain and suffering, will at last be raised into a realm of divine justice and benevolence. Personally, I find the idea of reincarnation a profoundly benevolent one.

Practical consequences

Another aspect of the idea of reincarnation and destiny relates to our tangible social existence together. It seems to me that this principle can enhance the 'resonance' of human encounters. Taking reincarnation into account can, for example, offer doctors, teachers and therapists a way of seeing an individual in a larger context. Thus, a teacher can be aware that the pupil standing in front of them brings with them a whole history, with their own intentions, tasks and abilities. This can strengthen the teacher's respect for the uniqueness and idiosyncrasies of the pupil, without any need to try to uncover details of their karma.

Taking up the idea of reincarnation might make it easier to reveal a deeper stratum in each human being. Each person then becomes an individuality who meets us in this life with physical and soul limitations, but within whom there lives an unimpaired spirit: one that comes from a specific past intrinsic to them and is journeying in continuous development towards a future of their own. This outlook could also stand as a defence against the abhorrent idea that some lives are of 'lesser value' because they have not followed a 'normal' path of human development, such as those with physical or mental disabilities. Indeed, that is a short-sighted view, for who knows what a 'disabled' person might not learn and achieve specifically because they have greater difficulties to overcome than others do? And what capacities might they be developing that we fail to recognise because they are not quantifiable from a mundane perspective?

'Après moi le déluge' becomes redundant

Finally, I want to consider these ideas from an ecological perspective. Much harmful human behaviour originates in the thoughtlessness with which we look to the future (or rather, fail to look to the future): it starts with the careless throwing away of plastic bags that will lie around on the earth for decades, and continues with the endless waste products of industry. Sadly, there is a widespread view that it doesn't matter what happens to the earth when we're gone: '*Après moi le déluge*,' as the saying goes, 'After me, the flood.' It is thought that the younger and future generations will sort out the mess and that our personal 'environmental sins' can be left to them to shoulder since we ourselves don't have so long to live. But if we pay heed to reincarnation, this changes everything. If we know that the consequences of our actions and inactions will be laid at our own door in future because they have a karmic connection with us – that, in whatever way this might happen, they will return to us – then we are likely to see our own 'ecological footprint' in a different way from someone for whom death is the absolute end of life.

To see our own existence as part of the destiny community that encompasses all of humanity, gives rise to an exalted conception of the idea of reincarnation. This 'humanity' becomes, through repeated earthly lives, suddenly more than an abstract totality. It is a reality to which each of us belongs and which each of us helps shape and fashion through our many lives on earth. The resigned despair of climate activists who speak of a 'last generation' cannot be the last word here. As all humanity we are involved in a journey of evolution in common with the earth: we need the earth and the earth needs us! And we will continue to need each other – earth and humanity – until, at the end of our many incarnations, we will enter into a new reality as yet wholly unimaginable, and to which even visionaries like Rudolf Steiner can do no more than point.

6. The Way Ahead

If, in conclusion, I try to sum up these reflections, I have to acknowledge that the dimensions of reincarnation and karma are so vast that, in relation to them, our understanding is still in its infancy. The unresolved questions outweigh any answers. It has become apparent that, to speak rationally of karma, I have often had to resort to the subjunctive – 'may be', 'could be'.

But we have mapped out a path. Through inner self-observation we can identify an irreducible 'I', a spirit-soul being. If we assume that this spirit-soul being also continues to exist after death in some way or other, then the idea of reincarnation represents a version of individual immortality that makes most sense. And if we then broaden our horizons to encompass the idea of world evolution, it becomes apparent that the further evolution of the human individual beyond birth and death acquires a profound meaning: the gradually evolving human spirit increasingly takes hold of itself in such a way as to enter into conscious connection with the spirit at work in reality, enabling that spirit to become individualised in us. Besides world evolution, an individual process of evolution is happening in every single one of us, giving rise to a spiritual lineage we ourselves bring forth that has never previously existed. Spiritual individualities emerge, not only as unique variations on a universal humanity (rather like the characteristic variants within single animal species), but as developing proponents of an increasingly 'humanised' spirituality, which could not occur without this individualisation. We could put it like this: if we consider the idea, characteristic of modernity, that all phenomena, from galaxies through to the origins of the earth and human beings, can be understood in terms of evolution, then the principle of reincarnation extends this concept to embrace multiple lives for individual human beings and humanity as a whole. Karma is the putty on this journey, the adhesive principle that combines all the mistakes and omissions connected with this evolution, along with all successful outcomes, and ensures that evolution continually progresses. We are only beginning to sense the degree to which our daily life is sustained by this largely unconscious putty.

The idea of reincarnation changes everything: it extends our worldview beyond a purely physical world of cause and effect, allowing us to see ourselves as spiritual beings and enhancing our sense of responsibility and connection with others. We are continually surrounded by the invisible networks of destiny, but its fine threads only become apparent to us in glimpses. They are woven from more than human morality and spirituality, which is why the rational mind must broaden itself to comprehend this greater reality. There is also a risk here, as we try to bridge the gulf of what we cannot yet understand, of sliding into speculation and succumbing to mere curiosity and self-deception.

But this much is clear: karma is not something romantic or sentimental, nor can it be understood with a purely rational, mechanistic form of thinking. It is connected with a quality of wisdom to which our daily awareness is scarcely equal, so it is hardly surprising if critics disparage the idea without even trying to comprehend it.

In a podcast conversation with Matze Hielscher, the philosopher Markus Gabriel once said he was sure there was such a thing as destiny because 'There's an end to Tinder at some point'. By which he meant that online dating platforms like Tinder will become superfluous once destiny has connected us with the right partner.

Markus Gabriel pointed to the phenomenon of synchronicity, that is, seemingly chance occurrences in our life that turn out to be deeply meaningful and fruitful, especially where important human relationships are concerned. All of us, surely, have had such experiences or at least know others who have – unexpected encounters due to delayed or missed trains, or a random glance at an advert, or passing comments from friends, which then led to life-changing developments. Markus Gabriel says that without such synchronicities, or at least without the workings of destiny, our lives would be wholly meaningless. And our feelings of familiarity with people whom we have only just met, or the manifold difficulties through which, eventually, something important for my life comes about – all this becomes more comprehensible when we entertain the possibility of destiny. To do so is to intuit a new stratum of our being that does not belong to us in the same way as our personal ego does, but which surrounds us as a network of all the factors that both hinder and sustain us in our lives – a kind of peripheral self that is interwoven with the world and its subtle processes.

I will end by reiterating this: reincarnation stands in the greatest conceivable contrast to reductionist science, which recognises only empirical data. From this perspective, nothing is better able to enlarge the prevailing worldview than the idea of reincarnation. Its future still awaits it.

Notes

Introduction
1. Gabriel, *Der Mensch als Tier* (*Man as an Animal*).

1. Reincarnation in East and West
   1. Obst, *Reinkarnation: Weltgeschichte einer Idee* (*Reincarnation: The History of an Idea*).
   2. See Matthew 11:14 and 17:10–13.
   3. See *Fragmente der Vorsokratiker*, edited by Wilhelm Capelle
   4. Plutarch, *Adversus Colotem*, Section 12.
   5. See Steiner, *Karmic Relationships: Esoteric Studies, Volume 3*, lecture of August 1, 1924.
   6. Bock, *Wiederholte Erdenleben* (*Repeated Earth Lives*).
   7. Lessing, *The Education of the Human Race*.
   8. Spicker, *Lessing's Weltanschauung* (*Lessing's Worldview*).
   9. Steiner, *Theosophy*, p.76.

2. The Challenges Posed by Reincarnation
   1. In a lecture he gave on February 9, 1912, Rudolf Steiner mentioned how a woman he had met recently had informed him that she had been Mary Magdalene in a previous incarnation. Steiner told his audience, 'I could only reply that she was the twenty-fourth Mary Magdalene I had met during my life!' See Steiner, *Esoteric Christianity*, p.253.
   2. Wilber, *The Religion of Tomorrow*.

3. Wilder, *The Eighth Day*.
4. Spicker, *Lessing's Weltanschauung* (*Lessing's Worldview*).
5. Steiner, *Christ and the Human Soul*, p. 155.
6. Tetens, *Gott denken. Ein Versuch über rationale Theologie* (*Thinking About God: An Essay On Rational Theology*).
7. Ibid.
8. Steiner, *Manifestations of Karma*, p. 65.
9. Steiner, *Christ and the Human Soul*, p. 155.

3. Freedom Seeks Karma
1. Steiner, *Theosophy*, p. 84.
2. Ibid., p. 87.
3. Ibid.
4. *Info3 extra*, 3/1987, p. 22.
5. Steiner, *Lucifer-Gnosis*, p. 371.
6. Ibid., p. 362.
7. Zotz, *Mit Buddha das Leben meistern* (*Mastering Life with Buddha*).
8. *Info3*, 3/2023.

4. Karma as Development Not Punishment
1. Steiner, *Manifestations of Karma*, p. 67.
2. Steiner, *Rosicrucian Wisdom*, p. 43.
3. Steiner, *Disease, Karma and Healing*, p. 169.
4. Steiner, *Die menschliche Seele in ihrem Zusammenhang mit göttlich-geistigen Individualitäten* (*The Human Soul and its Connection with the Divine-Spiritual Individuals*), p. 22.
5. Steiner, *Disease, Karma and Healing*, p. 140.

5. Karma Enhances Human Dignity
1. Goethe, in a conversation with Johann Peter Eckermann on February 4, 1829.
2. Goethe, in a conversation with Johannes Daniel Falk on January 25, 1813.

Bibliography

Bock, Emil, *Wiederholte Erdenleben: Die Wiederverkörperungsidee in der deutschen Geistesgeschichte* (*Repeated Earth Lives: The Idea of Reincarnation in German Intellectual History*), Urachhaus, Germany 1997.

Gabriel, Markus, *Der Mensch als Tier* (*Man as an Animal*), Ullstein Hardcover, Germany 2022.

Lamberty, Pia, and Nocun, Katharina, *Gefährlicher Glaube: Die radikale Gedankenwelt der Esoterik* (*Dangerous Belief: The Radical World of Esoteric Thought*), Quadriga, Germany 2022.

Lessing, Gotthold Lessing, *The Education of the Human Race*, Anodos Books, UK 2021.

Obst, Helmut, *Reinkarnation: Weltgeschichte einer Idee* (*Reincarnation: The History of an Idea*) C. H. Beck, Germany 2011.

Spicker, Gideon, *Lessing's Weltanschauung* (*Lessing's Worldview*), Hansebooks, Germany 2024.

Steiner, Rudolf, *An Esoteric Cosmology: Evolution, Christ and Modern Spirituality* (CW94), SteinerBooks, USA 2008.

—, *Christ and the Human Soul: The Meaning of Life; The Spiritual Foundation of Morality; Anthroposophy and Christianity* (CW155), SteinerBooks, USA 2023.

—, *Die menschliche Seele in ihrem Zusammenhang mit göttlich-geistigen Individualitäten. Die Verinnerlichung der Jahresfeste* (*The Human Soul and its Connection with the Divine-Spiritual Individuals. The Internalisation of the Festivals of the Year*) (GA224), Steiner Verlag, Switzerland 1966.

—, *Disease, Karma and Healing: Spiritual-Scientific Enquiries into the Nature of the Human Being* (CW107), Rudolf Steiner Press, UK 2014.

—, *Esoteric Christianity and the Mission of Christian Rosenkreutz* (CW130), Rudolf Steiner Press, UK 2005.

—, *Four Mystery Dramas* (CW14), SteinerBooks, USA 2007.

—, *Karmic Relationships: Esoteric Studies, Volume 3* (CW237), Rudolf Steiner Press, UK 1977.

—, *Lucifer-Gnosis: Grundlegende Aufsätze zur Anthroposophie und Berichte aus den Zeitschriften 'Luzifer' und 'Lucifer-Gnosis' 1903–1908* (*Lucifer-Gnosis: Foundational Essays on Anthroposophy and Reports from the Periodicals 'Lucifer' and 'Lucifer-Gnosis' 1903–1908*) (GA34), Steiner Verlag, Switzerland 1960.

—, *Manifestations of Karma* (CW120), Rudolf Steiner Press, UK 2011.

—, *Rosicrucian Wisdom: An Introduction* (CW99), Rudolf Steiner Press, UK 2000.

—, *Theosophy: An Introduction to the Spiritual Processes in Human Life and in the Cosmos* (CW9), Anthroposophic Press, USA 1994.

Tetens, Holm, *Gott denken, Ein Versuch* über *rationale Theologie* (*Thinking About God: An Essay On Rational Theology*), Reclam Verlag, Germany 2015

Wilber, Ken, *The Religion of Tomorrow: A Vision for the Future of the Great Traditions*, Shambhala Publications, USA 2018.

Zotz, Volker, *Mit Buddha das Leben meistern: Buddhismus für Praktiker* (*Mastering Life with Buddha: Buddhism for Practitioners*), Rowolt Taschenbuch, Germany 1999.

You may also be interested in...

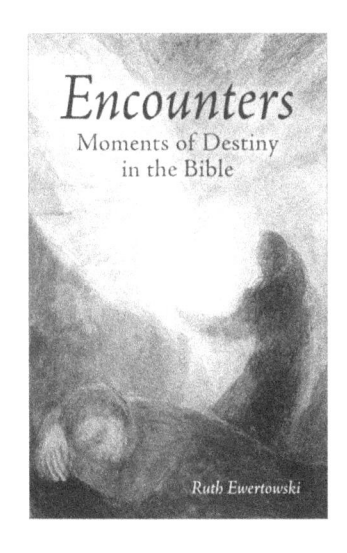

florisbooks.co.uk

Floris Books

For news on all our **latest books**,
and to receive **exclusive discounts**,
join our mailing list at:

florisbooks.co.uk

Plus subscribers get a FREE book
with every online order!

We will never pass your details to anyone else.